Building Constellations

Morgan Dakota

BookLeaf Publishing

India | USA | UK

Presentation by *BookLeaf Publishing*

Web: www.bookleafpub.com

E-mail: info@bookleafpub.com

ISBN: 9789357447904

First edition 2022

DEDICATION

Dedicated to my mother, who I hope knows I will always try to share my stars when hers get a bit too dim.

And in honor of my brother, my greatest loss, but my biggest inspiration. You were my first star.

ACKNOWLEDGEMENT

There's so many people that I want to acknowledge in life. So many who have believed in me endlessly and supported me consistently.

To my mother, Claire, and my sister, Cassi, who have always been there as pillars of strength and hope. Life has been cruel to us far too often, but I always know I can rely on you and your faith in me. Also, to my nephew, Dawson, who has become one of the very stars in my constellation. I love you all. Thank you for trusting me.

To Dr. Hall, one of the best professors and friends I have ever known. Your guidance is something I treasure dearly and I know I can always turn to you. Thank you for being such an inspiration. Even as a writer, I don't believe I have the words to ever truly convey what you mean to me. Just know I will always admire you and think you one of the smartest people I've ever met.

To my best friends: Alissa, Tara, Tia, Victoria, Rachel, Chey, Mayra, Logan. You all are so incredibly important to me. I cannot say how many times I've been grateful for your roles in my life. You've all been with me through some of the hardest moments, holding me up through it, and cheering me on. You've all been such cheerleaders when it comes to me writing anything, and I love you for that, but more than that, I love you for your friendship. You'll always be some of the people who make me laugh the loudest and the longest.

To the rest of my family: my dad, Johnny, my uncles, my grandparents, Aunt Mary, Anna. You've all been supporters since you knew I wanted to be a writer, knew I had words to share. Thank you for everything.

To Smo-Mo and Mrs. Bibler, thank you for being the teachers who I still cherish long after my tumultuous relationship with high school was over.

To the authors and writers who made me want to be one, I am who I am because of you.

To the bands and musicians who have gotten me through the hardest moments when no one else could, BTS, State Champs, and Halsey specifically, you held my hand through lyrics and taught me the most about not being alone. Thanks for being constellations in your own right.

PREFACE

Building Constellations came to be an idea of mine when I figured out that sometimes all it takes is a small amount of light to pull you out of a dark place, but the concept didn't really ring true for awhile. The reason being is that I was not always satisfied with just a small amount of light, with a single star. My world was far too dark for that one small beacon of hope to be nearly enough. Almost as though it were not real, I had to question why I had to cling to just one star. To question such a thing felt beyond selfish. When things were so dark, I should have been content to have that small piece of light shine on me.

As I've gotten older, having faced more and more darkness, new realities, and new pains, I realized that when it comes to finding your own peace, there's no such thing as selfishness. To want more light is not too much to ask of this world. It is not selfish to want to be okay, to be less alone.

Once I realized this, I knew it wouldn't come easily. That solitary light, that first star, it gave me just enough light, though. While not enough by itself, it shed just enough glow to help me search for the next star. It helped me realize that if I found enough light, I could build my own constellation. I couldn't deny building constellations wouldn't be enough to see by.

And even if stars occasionally burn out, even if I'm cast into shadows and darkness once again, maybe if I've built enough constellations, my universe will stay lit up long enough to build more.

Constellation 915

They mean so much,
Those stars of mine.
I've watched them dim,
I've seen them shine.

So far away,
Distant, it's true.
I've never felt more comfort
Than I have with you.

You've shared your lights,
You've held my heart.
I'm no longer afraid
Of what's in the dark.

Collapse

I collapsed the day your star did.
You fell from the sky,
And so did I.
The difference was,
I was not allowed.

I was not allowed,
To turn to dust.
I was not allowed to fall.
To crumble,
To crash.
I was expected to shine still.

I was expected,
To sparkle, to gleam.
To cast a light that-
That I wasn't sure belonged to me.
But I collapsed.

I collapsed.
I collided.
With the darkness,
That surrounded me.
I didn't shine.
My light went out.
Just like your star did.

But I'll try to shine,
For you if no one else.

Breathe

What is it to breathe?
To have things that are easy?
The weight bears down,
Claws at the chest,
Begging for release.
Here's to drowning on land.

A basic skill,
To function,
To live.
But it's out of reach.
It's grasping at straws.
It laughs as it stares.

Given these gifts that are inherent,
Only to lack them when needed.
A pretty present,
But far too much tape.
There was no affording it anyway.
Take a good look.

The moment you stop,
Let it trap you,
In that way it does,
Feet trapped in quicksand.
You lose, you sink.
You're in check.

But-
What is it to breathe?

Soulmates

Fast and brilliant with the way it burns,
Collapse is inevitable.
Restrained and gasping,
Breath is delectable.

You saw him, but you didn't know.
Didn't know he was the reason.
Connected and intertwined,
String of fate no longer weavin'.

Unimaginable how it happened,
The way you were brought together.
Should anything change? Can it?
No one knows better.

Bright, blinding,
Made of stardust, that boy.
He called you the sun,
His Helen of Troy.

Greater stories have been written.
Many deeper and more tragic.
But yours is the best,
It holds its own kind of magic.

Sometimes losing breath,
Sometimes causing tears.
But nothing is more precious,
Than the quiet moments held dear.

You're there for him,
And he for you.
The dust has settled,
In his arms, you're born anew.

Black and Blue

You didn't paint me black and blue,
But you crushed my spirit,
Brought forth tears,
And that hurt too.

Even when the names, the curses,
Weren't hurled my way,
They defined me,
You still had your say.

Pressed down so low,
Deeper and deeper under your thumb,
It was hard to grow,
It was hard to run.

You never hit me,
But you left marks.
I don't know when they'll heal,
Or where to start.

I gave you excuses,
Didn't think it was 'that bad,'
But the less I felt free,
All I know is sad-ness.

I didn't know I was a victim,
Not in this way.
But it should have been clear,
When I never wanted you to stay.

Icarus

Dust settled,
Patterns left behind,
In an afterthought.
Desolation.
The world is gone,
But you,
You were here.

I never knew what home was,
Until you.
Never knew what love was,
Until after.
I flew too close to the sun.
But it was nice to burn.

The Cracks

Many won't remember when time stopped.
They won't remember when the clocks cracked.
When the springs were sprung,
When every thing ceased and became still.

Many won't remember being lifted from bed,
Being sat down,
Being spoken to.
Always remembering the moment, but never the
words.

Most won't remember the confusion,
Being told to go back to sleep.
Being told to stand still.
Most won't remember being lifted by the wrong
hands.

Most won't remember the pain,
The lack of understanding.
The being unaware of how massive it all was.
Most won't remember how everything changed.

Most won't remember the deepest of blue,
The smile, the laughter.
The lack of time spent.
Most won't remember how you were pulled away.

Most won't remember the day that time stopped.
Sometimes, I don't.
Sometimes, I don't remember a lot of things.
But I remember that everything ceased only two days
away.

I remember the cracks.
I know I still live with them.

Only Here

The floor shakes,
Vibrations caused by the many hearts,
For once in tandem.
Only here do we bleed the same.

Battle cries escape,
The beating of drums,
Not enough to overpower the night.
Only here do we scream together.

Spells woven intricately, fly into the air,
Lights of varying color our war paint.
Magic that makes warriors, survivors.
Only here do we feel alive.

Only here do we feel united,
Despite our own experience with war.

It Always Comes Back

Slithering, seeping,
The blackness grows.
Oozing, smothering,
Not letting go.

Taking root, it eats away.
All that's left is remnants.
Once alive, but no longer.
Only decay is left, not descendants.

It seems okay,
For now, at least.
But soon, it'll return.
The monster will feast.

Stay Close To Me

Stay close to me.
I can hardly breathe.
Vision so clouded, can no longer see.
Down on my knees,
Again.

Stay close to me.
Praying, waiting, hoping.
Nothing changes.
But everything does.
Nothing will ever be the same.
What once was an "is" turns to a "was."

Stay close to me.
Always right there.
Yes, you left,
But I'm still right here.
Time moved on,
But I didn't.
I couldn't.

Stay close to me.
Never too far.
Still you linger,
Brighter than the stars.

Collecting there,
Like dust on a shelf.
Things have settled,
But in the stillness,
Yeah, there, I need help.

Stay close to me.
Don't you dare stray.
I want to open my eyes,
I want this to never fade.
Be there when it's too much.
Be within distance to clutch.

Stay close to me.
Stay within reach.
Stay right here,
So I can still speak.
Make these dreams,
Be a reality.
Stay so close,
I can hardly fathom it.

Just-
Stay.
Stay as close as you can.
Stay close to me.
Darling, continue to hold my hand.

What a Relief

In all the lifetimes,
Under all the possible skies,
They were made for each other.
Their own constellation.
Endlessly connected.

Maybe they weren't always together,
Maybe they didn't always recognize each other,
Maybe they just made it before the end,
Maybe the world wasn't ready then.

But, oh, how lucky are we,
To exist in the same time as them once they
found their way.
Because nothing has ever burned brighter.

In the Gray

I posted your photo today in black and white.
It seemed poetic somehow for you to live in the
gray.
I'll remember you in color, but your absence
lives on in that void between,
The lack of color and what is seen.

It's been years since I've seen you, but I
remember so well.
If I'm being honest, it's the pictures that keep
those memories at their strongest.
The blues, the greens, the pinks, and reds.
Oh, how you live in my head. In my chest.

I struggle to breathe more often than not.
I don't blame you. I wouldn't if I could.
Were you a catalyst?
Or do I bring this on?
Hold onto the pain, so you're no longer gone?

To Write

She closes her eyes,
But not to sleep.
Dream worlds await,
Dragging her down deep.

Swirling skies of blue,
Vibrant fields of green.
Strangers' faces,
The only thing seen.

It's right there,
Within grasp.
All she needs,
Is to ask.

To follow,
Wherever the path leads.
Grow the flowers,
That have planted seeds.

Adventure awaits!
Come explore!
If she merely,
Opens the door.

I Choose My Scars

I've inked my skin to remember.
To remember you,
To remember myself.
To learn.
Multiple times I chose pain willingly.
As to not let go of what I've known for so long.

It's in honor of you,
But then I remember the limited time.
The limited pictures not branded into my skin.
My art versus what was granted,
It's already older than you.
I've already known it much longer.
It's held onto me longer, grasped me tighter.
You didn't get to do that.
My art has had more of a choice than any of us.

And I no longer know if my art is for you or for
me.
I just had to have something.
Something that would stay longer.
Longer than you were allowed to.
I had to choose the scars that people could see,
Because they can't always see the ones within
me.

Masked

If I show you a mask,
You have no choice but to believe it.
Even if pulled back,
Are you done being deceived yet?

Sharp edges, bright colors,
Glued together, I'm a masterpiece.
A story that's molded by tragedy,
Still, you'll see what you want to see.

I'll tell you one thing,
Because I know you're not ready.
No one is willing,
To be given truths quite so heavy.

On the surface,
Everything is fine.
Whether I'm playing a part,
Or you're simply ignoring the signs.

And of course, no one wants to know,
But the world is quite ugly.
So, if you ask, I can tell,
Or keep it under lock and key.

Because the simple truth is,
You only accept hideous things,
When you're also the one,
Who is no longer holding any strings.

Drowning

Beaten down by the constant wave,
Reaching up is the only thing she could do.
Grasping, reaching, hoping for a save.
Forever forgetting to hold the last breath she
clung to.
Lungs constantly screaming, heart forever
bleeding,
Never actually alone, but not seeing
Drowning is never a solitary sport.

Sometimes one drowns and there's nothing to be
done.
Oh, how she wishes she could have saved
herself,
But sometimes all there is left to do is save
someone
Else. Never alone in her screaming,
There's always an echo of another scream out
there.

The Fairy Tale

Once upon a time,
That's how the stories always start.
There's a boy, a girl,
A tale woven about winning the other's heart.

It all seems romantic.
We're taught it's what should be.
But what happens when-
When ourselves isn't what we see.

The princess is in danger!
A dragon! A tower!
Only a prince can save her!
But men make her cower...

But- even if, if men weren't her problem?
Why is it that it's only okay,
For them to save her?
Does it absolve them?

They write the stories,
Expect you to read them.
She never had a choice,
But to believe him.

Pride

Taught to hate everything that I am,
Society says this, says that,
Morality is based on who speaks the loudest.

But there's whispers,
The little voice inside,
Only when I trust me is it proudest.

Eventually, there will be nowhere to hide.
No one should have to.
And that's why I have pride.

Caged

Does it whisper to you?
Does it suggest there's more?
That voice inside,
Begging to soar.

It's in a cage,
Locked up tight.
Only our true selves,
Are let out at night.

Because the world is quiet,
There's nothing to hear.
And when it's quiet,
There's less to fear.

Just For You

"I love you, but-"
But- but what?
Why isn't it enough?
Why is it too much?

It's too much to love,
Too much to ask.
Too much to love,
Without requesting less.

Requesting different.
Expected to change,
To bend, to meld,
Into your ideas.

Your ideas of what one is,
What one needs to be.
Because it's too much,
To simply love me.

You love me, but-
But I must be different.
I must change to fit.
To fit your ideas of what love is.

Because somehow,
It's my problem that you're incapable.
It's my fault that you don't,
That you can't love simply.

It's my fault for loving who I am,
My fault for refusing to,
For not becoming someone else,
Just for you.

I Know Me

"Why can't you be okay?"
A question I've asked myself,
Been asked myself,
Overheard myself.

"Why aren't you happy?"
A similar inquiry.
It comes from the same people.
The ones who also aren't happy.

"When will you get better?"
Like it's the flu.
Like it goes away.
Like there's something I can do.

Yes, I ask myself these questions too,
But I am aware,
I know,
This will always be there.

It's not going away,
I'm not going to be magically healed.
But over time,
I will learn how to deal.

So, sorry,
So sorry,
If it's not good enough,
If it's not- If I'm not?

I'm not that sorry.
No, not really.
This is how I exist.
I don't need the pity.

It isn't pretty,
It isn't perfect.
I hate it enough for both of us,
Your words aren't worth it.

But I'm still here.
I'm here,
And I understand.
I know who I am.

I know the world isn't easy,
I know what it is to breathe.
I know, I know,
It's strange to see.

But maybe-
Just maybe,
You'll believe,
That you don't know me better than I know me.

Because, while these questions?
They make sense,
But it's unfair to ask.
Unfair for you to think you have a better grasp.

I can question myself,
But you shouldn't.
Not when I'm doing,
What you're saying you couldn't.